GOD, WHAT'S THE HOLD UP?

How the state
of the World Today
Aligns with the Bible's
End Times Prophecies

GARY PAUL GATES
FOREWORD BY DERRICK DREW

"So thou, O son of man, I have set thee a watchman unto the house of Israel; therefore thou shalt hear the word at my mouth, and warn them from me."

-Ezekiel 33:7

Dedication

This book is lovingly dedicated to the faithful messengers who continue to sound the alarm—those who, with courage and conviction, proclaim the truth of what is to come. Some of you stand week after week behind pulpits in churches around the world. Others reach hearts through a digital screen, sharing the gospel with a cell phone in hand or a webcam as your platform. Some walk the streets, knock on doors, and meet people where they are. However you choose to share the Good News, know this: I see you. I honor you. And I thank you. You are watchmen and watchwomen—called, courageous, and committed. Together, we are united in purpose: to lift up the name of Jesus and point others to His soon return.

This book is also dedicated to you, the reader. Whether you've opened these pages as a warning before the great disappearance of Christ-followers in the rapture—or you've found it in the midst of chaos and confusion—know this: you are not forgotten, and you are not without hope. My prayer is that these words will minister to your heart, open your eyes, and lead you to the truth. If I am no longer here when you read this, let it be known—I wrote this with you in mind. Jesus is still reaching for you. And as long as you have breath, it is not too late to receive Him.

–Gary Paul Gates

Copyright © Gary Paul Gates 2025
All rights reserved.

Paperback ISBN: 9798281087841
Hardback ISBN: 9798281089074

Bible References are from The Holy Bible:
King James Version (KJV), Public Domain

*More books available,
including children's books:*
www.itsnotsorandom.com

Table of Contents

Foreword by Derrick Drew   7
Introduction: "God, What's the Hold Up?"   13

Part 1: The Signs Are Everywhere
- **Chapter 1: The Dream That Shook Me**   15
- **Chapter 2: When the Bible Looks Like the News**   19
- **Chapter 3: The Chastisement Wake-Up Call**   23

Part 2: The Rapture is Real—and Close
- **Chapter 4: Pre-Tribulation Hope**   27
- **Chapter 5: What Happens Next**   31
- **Chapter 6: This is Not a Drill**   35

Part 3: Living with Urgency
- **Chapter 7: Heaven is Free—But Not Cheap**   39
- **Chapter 8: Shouting from the Rooftops**   43
- **Chapter 9: When the Belief Becomes Sight**   47

Conclusion: This is It
- **Chapter 10: The Invitation**   51

In-Depth Reflections   55

> "He has not forgotten us. He is still coming for us."
>
> –Derrick Drew

Foreword
Beating the Odds
by Derrick Drew

"Knowing this first, that there shall come in the last days scoffers, walking after their own lusts, and saying, Where is the promise of his coming? for since the fathers fell asleep, all things continue as they were from the beginning of the creation."
— 2 Peter 3:3–4 (KJV)

We don't know exactly what year the crucifixion took place, but tradition places it around 33 AD. While we can't be certain, if that timeline is accurate, then here in the year 2025, it has been approximately **1,992 years** since Jesus left this earth. And so, the scoffers say, "It's been nearly 2,000 years and Jesus hasn't returned yet. What makes you Christians think He's still coming back? Give it up."

In one sense, they seem to have a point—**if** you're looking at this from a strictly human perspective. The odds, from that viewpoint, would appear to be 1,992 to 1 against Jesus returning in any given year. If He doesn't come in 2025, those odds grow to 1,993 to 1 in 2026, and so on. Year by year, the odds seem to stretch further and further away.

That's why I love the title of Gary's new book: *"God, What's the Hold Up?"* Because let's be honest—every Christian, even the seasoned and spiritually mature, has probably felt that way at some point.

The odds of Jesus returning might seem to grow with each passing day. But as Han Solo once famously said in *Star Wars*, "Never tell me the odds, kid!"

Because here's the truth—**Jesus has already beaten the odds.**

Scholars estimate that at His first coming, Jesus fulfilled at least 300, and possibly as many as 570, Old Testament prophecies. Some are very familiar to us, such as the prophecy about the Messiah being born in Bethlehem:

> *"But thou, Bethlehem Ephratah, though thou be little among the thousands of Judah, yet out of thee shall he come forth unto me that is to be ruler in Israel; whose goings forth have been from of old, from everlasting."*
> — Micah 5:2 (KJV)

Or the one about the King riding into Jerusalem on Palm Sunday:

> *"Rejoice greatly, O daughter of Zion; shout, O daughter of Jerusalem: behold, thy King cometh unto thee: he is just, and having salvation; lowly, and riding upon an ass, and upon a colt the foal of an ass."*
> — Zechariah 9:9 (KJV)

These are just two of **hundreds** of Old Testament prophecies Jesus fulfilled at His first coming. Someone once calculated the probability of one person fulfilling just **eight** of those major prophecies. The odds?

1 in 100,000,000,000,000,000.

To put that into perspective: Imagine the entire state of

Texas covered in silver dollars two feet deep. One of those coins is marked. All the coins are mixed, and a blindfolded man is told to pick one coin—just **one**—on his first try. The chances of him grabbing the right one are the same odds as Jesus fulfilling just **eight** of the sixty major prophecies. But He didn't just fulfill eight—**He fulfilled them all.** The probability of Jesus **not** being the Messiah is mathematically impossible.

(Source: *More Than a Carpenter*, Josh McDowell. Submitted by the Homiletics class of West Coast Baptist College)

So yes, it's been 1,992 years since Jesus ascended into Heaven. But when you weigh that against the odds He already beat—**1 in 100 quadrillion**—suddenly, those scoffers don't seem so convincing. Jesus already beat the odds once, and He'll do it again.

So, if you ever wonder what's taking Him so long, take comfort in His own words:

> *"Let not your heart be troubled: ye believe in God, believe also in me.*
> *In my Father's house are many mansions: if it were not so, I would have told you.*
> *I go to prepare a place for you.*
> *And if I go and prepare a place for you, I will come again, and receive you unto myself;*
> *that where I am, there ye may be also.*
> *And whither I go ye know, and the way ye know."*
> — John 14:1–4 (KJV)

He has **not** forgotten us. He **is** still coming for us.

And for the scoffers stuck on the "2,000 years" argument, I invite you to keep reading in 2 Peter 3:

> *"For this they willingly are ignorant of, that by the word of God the heavens were of old...*
> *But, beloved, be not ignorant of this one thing, that one*

> *day is with the Lord as a thousand years,*
> *and a thousand years as one day.*
> *The Lord is not slack concerning his promise, as some men count slackness;*
> *but is longsuffering to us-ward, not willing that any should perish, but that all should come to repentance."*
> — 2 Peter 3:5–9 (KJV)

So why the delay?

Because of His great mercy.

God knows that your **odds of survival** in the Great Tribulation are not good. Consider just the beginning of it, described in Revelation 6:8:

> *"And I looked, and behold a pale horse: and his name that sat on him was Death, and Hell followed with him.*
> *And power was given unto them over the fourth part of the earth,*
> *to kill with sword, and with hunger, and with death, and with the beasts of the earth."*
> — Revelation 6:8 (KJV)

Right out of the gate, your chances of surviving drop—**1 in 4** will not make it past the fourth seal. How do you like those odds?

But here's the good news: **You don't have to be here for that.**

Though it seems like Jesus is taking a long time, the signs suggest His return is soon. That's the heart behind Gary's book—to encourage you that Jesus has already beaten the odds. He is **risen**, and He **is** coming soon. And you can be with Him. You don't have to go through the horrors of the Tribulation.

Gary will explain how before you reach the end of this book. So take your time. Soak it in. And when you finish—**get it into the hands of someone you love**.

Will you be an **overcomer**? Will you be one of those who beats the odds?

I may not know you, but I love you—because **Jesus loves you.** And I hope you're one of those overcomers. I hope I get to meet you soon—**in the clouds.**

–Foreword by Derrick (aka "The Long-Winded Preacher")
Host of Bible Study with Derrick

Visit Derrick's YouTube page:
https://www.youtube.com/@biblestudywithderrick

Visit Derrick's Rumble page:
https://rumble.com/user/BiblestudywithDerrick

"This book is my rooftop. These words are my shout."

–*Gary Paul Gates*

Introduction
God, What's the Hold Up?

I've lost count of how many times I've read the Bible, then turned on the news and felt a chill run down my spine. It's as if the headlines are reading straight out of Scripture. Each year, the resemblance grows stronger. The warnings become clearer. The clock ticks louder. And deep within my spirit, a question has often surfaced—not in doubt, but in desperation: *God, what's the hold up?*

A few years ago, I had a dream that's never left me. It was vivid. Startling. Prophetic. I was outside on the phone when something in the sky caught my attention. A light—bright, orange, white—cut through the darkness like a sword. A trumpet sounded, and before I could even process it, I was being pulled upward. My body passed through my phone and clothes, and an overwhelming peace washed over me. I wasn't human anymore—I was transformed. Drawn into a light that words can't describe. I woke up trembling.

Was it just a dream? A warning? A taste of what's to come? All I know is this: it marked me.

Since then, I can't shake the sense that we're moments away. The contractions are close. The birth pains are undeniable. The world is groaning, prophecy is unfolding, and Heaven is whispering one word louder than ever: *urgency.*

This book is my rooftop. These words are my shout. I'm not

writing to scare you—I'm writing to prepare you. I believe in the pre-tribulation rapture. I believe Jesus is coming back before the storm breaks loose. And I believe He's giving us a final moment to get real, wake up, and shine like we've never shined before.

If you've felt a strange pull in your spirit...

If the world feels too loud and your soul feels too homesick...

If you've wondered if we're running out of time...

You're not alone.

This is it.

The world may be blind to it. Many churches may be silent about it. But Heaven isn't quiet. The King is on His way. And when He comes, everything will change in the blink of an eye.

Let's get ready.

Let's stay watchful.

Let's sound the alarm while there's still time.

Because one day soon, we won't be here to say another word.

And if you're reading this after that day...

...then you know: we were right (said in humble desperation and compassion – not arrogance).

1
Chapter One
The Dream That Shook Me

It was just a few moments long—but it's never left me.

I was outside at night, talking on the phone with a friend. Nothing felt unusual. The air was calm. My thoughts were occupied with the conversation, just another ordinary moment in an ordinary day.

Then something caught my eye—something in the sky.

A light pierced the darkness. Bright. Orange. White. Like a flame with a heartbeat. It didn't fade in—it exploded into view. It felt alive. And then I heard it: a sound like a trumpet, vibrating the air and shaking something deep in my soul.

"This is it," I said.

And then it happened.

In a split second, my body was no longer responding to gravity. I felt a force pulling me upward—fast. My phone slipped through my hand. Not out of my hand, but *through* it, like my body had become something new. I looked down and saw my clothes falling to the ground as I was being drawn into the light.

What I felt in that moment can't fully be described in earthly terms. It was as if every worry, fear, and insecurity I ever carried was ripped from me. My human limitations were shedding like old skin. I was changing. Being transformed. Not just in body, but in being.

I wasn't floating—I was being claimed.

There was a calmness in that light I had never felt before. It wasn't the peace you get from a quiet day or a warm moment. It was supernatural. Complete. Final. It was as if I had come home.

And then I woke up.

I sat up in bed, shaken. Trembling. My heart was pounding with something deeper than fear—*urgency.*

Was it a warning? A glimpse of what's coming? Just something I ate the night before?

I don't believe in coincidences. And I know that dream was from God.

For months leading up to it, I'd been thinking constantly about the rapture. I had been consumed with the thought: *Jesus is coming soon.* I didn't know when. I still don't. But I can't shake the feeling—it's near. Closer than we think.

The Bible says in **1 Thessalonians 4:16–17 (KJV):**

"For the Lord himself shall descend from heaven with a shout, with the voice of the archangel, and with the trump of God: and the dead in Christ shall rise first: Then we which are alive and remain shall be caught up together with them in the clouds, to meet the Lord in the air: and so shall we ever be with the Lord."

That's exactly what I saw in my dream. And that's what I believe is about to happen.

Jesus also said in **Luke 21:36 (KJV):**

"Watch ye therefore, and pray always, that ye may be accounted worthy to escape all these things that shall come to pass, and to stand before the Son of man."

The warnings are clear. The signs are multiplying. And the question I now ask you is the same one I asked myself after that dream: **If it happened right now... would you be ready?**

Would your soul leap with joy and say, "This is it!" Or would your heart break with regret and say, "Oh no... they were right"?

1 Corinthians 15:52 (KJV) says:

"In a moment, in the twinkling of an eye, at the last trump: for the trumpet shall sound, and the dead shall be raised incorruptible, and we shall be changed."

That change is coming. The trumpet is going to sound. And when it does, everything we know will shift in an instant.

I don't write this chapter lightly. I write it with trembling hands and a heart full of urgency. If this dream was a glimpse of what's coming, then I can't keep it to myself. I don't want you to be left behind. I don't want you to miss the moment that changes everything.

We are living on the edge of eternity. And in the blink of an eye, we'll step into it.

This is it.

Let's make sure we're ready.

"The truth is, if your Bible looks like your news feed, then your spirit should be on high alert."

2
Chapter Two
When the Bible Looks Like News

I used to think people were exaggerating when they said, *"We're living in the last days."* Now, I think we're living in the last moments.

It's almost unsettling how Scripture mirrors our current reality. You turn on the news and see war, division, lawlessness, betrayal, and spiritual compromise—and then you read the Bible and find the same words staring back at you like a reflection in the mirror.

2 Timothy 3:1–5 (KJV) isn't just a passage anymore. It's a headline:

"This know also, that in the last days perilous times shall come. For men shall be lovers of their own selves, covetous, boasters, proud, blasphemers, disobedient to parents, unthankful, unholy, without natural affection, trucebreakers, false accusers, incontinent, fierce, despisers of those that are good, traitors, heady, highminded, lovers of pleasures more than lovers of God; having a form of godliness, but denying the power thereof: from such turn away."

We're not waiting for this to happen. We're living in it.

We've become a generation that celebrates self over sacrifice, money over morality, and pleasure over purpose. We binge chaos like entertainment, scroll past suffering, and dismiss the sacred as outdated. The very things the Bible said would mark the end are now the fabric of daily life.

Even the church isn't immune. Many pulpits have gone silent about sin. Prophecy is treated as optional. Urgency has been replaced by entertainment, and holiness has been exchanged for popularity. It's a dangerous shift.

But none of this surprises God. Jesus warned us plainly.

Matthew 24:6–8 (KJV):

"And ye shall hear of wars and rumours of wars: see that ye be not troubled: for all these things must come to pass, but the end is not yet. For nation shall rise against nation, and kingdom against kingdom: and there shall be famines, and pestilences, and earthquakes, in divers places. All these are the beginning of sorrows."

Sound familiar?

Earthquakes. Wars. Pandemics. Global unrest. We don't need a prophet to tell us—we need eyes to see what the Word already said.

I believe the reason these signs are increasing in frequency and intensity is because we're in the final stage. Like birth pains, they grow more intense and closer together as delivery nears.

And yet… so many are still asleep.

Even those who believe Jesus is coming are tempted to hit the spiritual snooze button. We tell ourselves we have more time. That we'll get serious later. But *later* is disappearing fast.

Romans 13:11 (KJV) says it best:

"And that, knowing the time, that now it is high time to awake out of sleep: for now is our salvation nearer than when we believed."

The truth is, *if your Bible looks like your news feed,* then your spirit should be on high alert.

We've been warned. We've been told what to watch for. And now we're seeing it unfold in real time.

It's not just the world that needs to wake up—*it's the church.*

Now is the time to get our house in order. Now is the time to live like He's coming today—because He very well could.

The question isn't *if* we're in the last days. The question is: *what are we doing with the time we have left?*

"God has used chastisement —not to destroy me, but to wake me up. To bring me back. To remind me that I was never created to be comfortable in this world."

3
Chapter Three
The Chastisement Wake-Up Call

Why does it take pain to make me pray? Why do I wait until everything is stripped away before I seek God like He's all I have—when He's all I ever needed?

It's not that I don't believe. I do. But I've come to see that belief and desperation are not always the same thing. Desperation changes the posture of your soul. It bends your knees and breaks your pride.

Sometimes, I wonder why I didn't bow sooner.

The truth is, God has used chastisement—not to destroy me, but to wake me up. To bring me back. To remind me that I was never created to be comfortable in this world.

Hebrews 12:6–7 (KJV) says:

"For whom the Lord loveth he chasteneth, and scourgeth every son whom he receiveth. If ye endure chastening, God dealeth with you as with sons; for what son is he whom the father chasteneth not?"

Chastisement is always looked at as just punishment—it's also proof of sonship.

It's not wrath—it's refinement. God loves us too much to let us drift into spiritual sleep without trying to shake us awake.

There have been seasons when I lost people I loved. Times

when doors slammed shut. When money ran out. When I was stripped down to nothing but questions and tears. And in every one of those valleys, I discovered a God who was never absent—just waiting for me to reach.

It's in those low places that He speaks most clearly.

Psalm 34:18 (KJV) says:

*"The Lord is nigh unto them that are of a broken heart;
and saveth such as be of a contrite spirit."*

The valley may have crushed me—but it didn't kill me. Because even there, I was not alone.

Maybe that's where you are right now—crushed, confused, barely holding on. You're not here by accident. The pain isn't pointless. God is trying to get your attention.

It shouldn't take loss to make us listen. It shouldn't take desperation to make us desperate for Him.

But sometimes… it does.

Deuteronomy 8:2 (KJV) reminds us:

*"And thou shalt remember all the way which the Lord
thy God led thee these forty years in the wilderness, to
humble thee, and to prove thee, to know what was in
thine heart, whether thou wouldest keep his command-
ments, or no."*

The wilderness wasn't just about punishment. It was about preparation too. And sometimes God allows a wilderness to show us what's really in our hearts—and to prove that even there, He is still God.

I've come to learn that chastisement is often the last warning before the trumpet. It's God saying, *"Come home before it's too late."*

He doesn't want us living on the edge of lukewarm. He doesn't want us scrolling ourselves into spiritual slumber. He wants us watching. Waiting. Burning with urgency.

Because when Jesus comes back, there won't be time to get ready—we must *be* ready.

Revelation 3:19 (KJV) says:

"As many as I love, I rebuke and chasten: be zealous therefore, and repent."

This is your wake-up call. Not because God is mad at you—but because He loves you too much to leave you the way you are.

If your life feels like it's shaking, don't curse the shaking—thank God for it. It may be the very thing that brings you to your knees…Right where your breakthrough begins.

"The rapture is not just a doctrine. It's a declaration that our Redeemer is coming for us."

4
Chapter Four
Pre-Tribulation Hope

The world is shaking.

Prophecy is unfolding.

And the question being asked more and more is: *"What happens next?"*

If you've ever studied the Bible with your eyes wide open, you've likely come across terms that can be described as **"the rapture."** It may seem controversial to some, but for those who believe in the authority of God's Word, it's not just a concept—it's a *promise*.

I believe in the **pre-tribulation rapture**—the belief that Jesus will call His church home *before* the seven-year tribulation begins. This isn't wishful thinking or escapism. It's *biblical hope* anchored in God's mercy and truth.

Let me show you why.

The Rapture Described

The most detailed description of the rapture is found in **1 Thessalonians 4:16–17 (KJV):**

"For the Lord himself shall descend from heaven with a shout, with the voice of the archangel, and with the trump of God: and the dead in Christ shall rise first:

Then we which are alive and remain shall be caught up together with them in the clouds, to meet the Lord in the air: and so shall we ever be with the Lord."

Paul doesn't say Jesus will come *to the earth*—he says we will meet Him *in the air.* This "catching away" of believers is sudden, supernatural, and global. It will happen "in a moment, in the twinkling of an eye" (**1 Corinthians 15:52**).

Not Appointed to Wrath

One of the strongest biblical supports for a pre-trib rapture is this: **God does not pour out His wrath on His bride.**

1 Thessalonians 5:9 (KJV) says:

"For God hath not appointed us to wrath, but to obtain salvation by our Lord Jesus Christ."

The tribulation isn't just a time of global suffering—it is the outpouring of God's wrath on a world that has rejected Him. But just like Noah was lifted above the flood and Lot was removed from Sodom, God has a history of removing the righteous before judgment falls.

A Promise to Escape

Jesus Himself said in **Luke 21:36 (KJV):**

"Watch ye therefore, and pray always, that ye may be accounted worthy to escape all these things that shall come to pass, and to stand before the Son of man."

"Escape all these things." That's a direct reference to the chaos He described in Luke 21—famines, earthquakes, betrayal, persecution, signs in the heavens, and distress among nations. Jesus doesn't say endure it. He says be ready to escape it.

Kept from the Hour

In Revelation, Jesus gives a promise to the faithful church in Philadelphia:

Revelation 3:10 (KJV):

"Because thou hast kept the word of my patience, I also will keep thee from the hour of temptation, which shall come upon all the world, to try them that dwell upon the earth."

He doesn't say *through* the hour—but *from* it. That phrase *"keep thee from"* in Greek literally means *"to take out of, away from."* This is not survival—it's removal.

Hope, Not Fear

The rapture is not something to fear. It's something to long for. Paul said in **Titus 2:13 (KJV):**

"Looking for that blessed hope, and the glorious appearing of the great God and our Saviour Jesus Christ."

The tribulation is real. The Antichrist is coming. But the church will not be here for the wrath of God. We have a *blessed hope*—not a dreadful fate.

What Does This Mean for Us Now?

It means we must be ready.

Not preparing out of fear, but out of faith. Not retreating, but reaching—telling everyone we can that Jesus is coming soon. And when He does, it will happen suddenly.

There won't be time to repent after the trumpet sounds. There won't be time to finally get serious about your walk with God. You will either go in the rapture—or face the greatest judgment the world has ever known.

But you don't have to wonder. You don't have to guess. You can be ready—right now.

The rapture is not just a doctrine. It's a declaration that *our Redeemer is coming for us.*

And it could happen at any moment.

This is it.

Let's be watching.

"Don't wait for the tribulation to wake you up. Don't gamble with your eternity. Jesus is coming. And the wrath that follows is not meant for you —but you must choose to escape it."

5
Chapter Five
What Will Happen During the Tribulation

If the rapture of the church happens before the tribulation—what comes next?

The answer is terrifying, and yet completely avoidable. It's called the **Tribulation**, a seven-year period of chaos, deception, judgment, and wrath like the world has never seen.

Jesus Himself warned in Matthew 24:21 (KJV):

"For then shall be great tribulation, such as was not since the beginning of the world to this time, no, nor ever shall be."

The tribulation will be divided into two parts: the first 3½ years of false peace and rising deception, followed by 3½ years of intense wrath, global catastrophe, and demonic destruction known as the **Great Tribulation**.

The Rise of the Antichrist

After the rapture, the world will be thrown into confusion. That's when a political and spiritual figure—**the Antichrist**—will rise with promises of peace, unity, and solutions to the global chaos.

2 Thessalonians 2:3–4 (KJV) warns:

"Let no man deceive you by any means: for that day shall not come, except there come a falling away first,

and that man of sin be revealed, the son of perdition; Who opposeth and exalteth himself above all that is called God, or that is worshipped; so that he as God sitteth in the temple of God, shewing himself that he is God."

He will deceive the nations, establish a one-world government, and eventually demand worship.

Judgments from Heaven

The Book of Revelation describes a series of divine judgments poured out upon the earth—*seals, trumpets, and vials*. These are not symbolic. They are literal acts of wrath.

Revelation 6 speaks of:
- Global war
- Economic collapse
- Widespread death
- Famine
- Cosmic disturbances

Revelation 8 and 9 describe:
- Fire falling from heaven
- A third of the earth burned
- Rivers turned bitter
- Demonic locusts tormenting mankind for five months
- A third of humanity wiped out

And by **Revelation 16**, we see the **vial judgments**, where:
- The sea turns to blood
- Painful sores cover people's bodies
- The sun scorches men with great heat
- Darkness falls on the Antichrist's kingdom
- The Euphrates River dries up for war
- And finally, the greatest earthquake in history strikes the planet

Persecution of Tribulation Saints

Some will come to faith during the tribulation—but they will pay a high price. These believers, often called "tribulation saints," will be hunted, persecuted, and martyred for refusing to worship the Antichrist or take his mark.

Revelation 13:16–17 (KJV) warns:

"And he causeth all, both small and great, rich and poor, free and bond, to receive a mark in their right hand, or in their foreheads: And that no man might buy or sell, save he that had the mark, or the name of the beast, or the number of his name."

To survive without this mark will be nearly impossible. But to receive it is to seal your fate.

A Final Chance—But a Terrible Cost

The tribulation is both judgment and mercy. It's God's final effort to bring repentance before the return of Christ to the earth.

But why face all of that, when you could *escape all these things* through faith in Jesus now?

Isaiah 55:6 (KJV) says:

"Seek ye the Lord while he may be found, call ye upon him while he is near."

The tribulation is not something to delay preparing for. You don't want to be here.

And if you think this world is hard now—just imagine it without the Holy Spirit's restraint, without the church's presence, and under the rule of a man possessed by Satan himself.

Today Is the Day

If you're reading this before the rapture, you still have time. If you're reading it after… your time is short.

But either way, God's message is clear:

2 Corinthians 6:2 (KJV):

"…behold, now is the accepted time; behold, now is the

day of salvation."

Don't wait for the tribulation to wake you up. Don't gamble with your eternity.

Jesus is coming. And the wrath that follows is not meant for you—but you must choose to escape it.

This is it.

Make sure you're ready before the door shuts.

6
Chapter Six
This Is Not a Drill

Have you ever slept through your alarm?

It goes off. It buzzes. It vibrates. You hit snooze—*just five more minutes.*

But eventually, reality catches up. You open your eyes and realize—you overslept. You're late. You missed your moment. The alarm was real, and now, so are the consequences.

That's where I believe much of the church is right now.

Spiritually drowsy.

Hitting snooze on prophecy.

Comfortable in chaos.

As if all of this—wars, lawlessness, shaking economies, moral collapse—is just one big practice run.

But let me say this as clearly as I can:

This is not a drill.

The signs aren't rehearsals. The trumpet isn't a test tone. The warnings are not dramatizations. We are in the final moments before Jesus returns for His bride.

Romans 13:11 (KJV) says:

"And that, knowing the time, that now it is high time to awake out of sleep: for now is our salvation nearer than when we believed."

The alarm has been sounding. And yet many have rolled over, pulled the covers tighter, and convinced themselves there's still time.

The Danger of Delay

Spiritual procrastination is a trap. It whispers, *"You've got time."* It suggests you can get serious about God later—after the next party, after the next success, after you've "lived your life."

But the Bible gives us **no guarantee** of a next moment.

Proverbs 27:1 (KJV) warns:

"Boast not thyself of to morrow;
for thou knowest not what a day may bring forth."

Tomorrow is not promised. But eternity is certain.

The rapture will not wait for your schedule. It will not accommodate your delays. When the trumpet sounds—it's over.

The Wise and the Foolish

Jesus gave a parable in **Matthew 25** about ten virgins—five wise, five foolish.

Matthew 25:6–10 (KJV):

"And at midnight there was a cry made, Behold, the
bridegroom cometh; go ye out to meet him. Then all
those virgins arose, and trimmed their lamps. And the
foolish said unto the wise, Give us of your oil; for our
lamps are gone out. But the wise answered, saying, Not
so; lest there be not enough for us and you: but go ye
rather to them that sell, and buy for yourselves. And
while they went to buy, the bridegroom came; and they
that were ready went in with him to the marriage: and
the door was shut."

The door was shut.

They weren't wicked. They weren't openly rebellious. They were just *unprepared*.

That's the danger of spiritual delay—it doesn't feel like rebellion.

It just feels like "not yet."

But when the moment comes, "not yet" becomes "too late."

False Alarms and Real Labor Pains

Some people say, *"We've heard this for years. People thought the world was ending decades ago."*

Yes—but that doesn't change the fact that we're closer now than ever before.

2 Peter 3:3–4 (KJV) says:

"There shall come in the last days scoffers, walking after their own lusts, And saying, Where is the promise of his coming? For since the fathers fell asleep, all things continue as they were from the beginning of the creation."

Scoffing at prophecy is part of prophecy.

The more people yawn at Jesus' return, the more likely it is we're nearing the day.

Just like contractions before childbirth, what we're seeing now—earthquakes, wars, famines, deception, division, and delusion—are not false alarms. They are labor pains. And when they reach full intensity, *delivery is coming.*

Get Ready—For Real

This chapter is your moment.

Your wake-up call.

Your "no more snooze button" moment.

If you've been lukewarm—*get on fire* If you've been drifting—*come back home.* If you've been watching the world fall apart but haven't surrendered your life to Christ—*today is the day.*

Because one day soon, the sky will split. The trumpet will sound. And every eye that was watching will lift upward and say…

"This is it."

> "Living Like We're Already There! If Heaven lives in you, it should show."

7
Chapter Seven
Heaven Is Free -But Not Cheap

Salvation doesn't cost us anything—But it cost Jesus *everything*.

Heaven is the free gift of God. It cannot be earned, bought, or inherited by good deeds. But let's not confuse *free* with *cheap*.

The cross wasn't painless. Grace wasn't effortless. The blood that washed away your sin came at the highest price imaginable: the death of the sinless Son of God.

Romans 6:23 (KJV) says:

"For the wages of sin is death; but the gift of God is eternal life through Jesus Christ our Lord."

The gift is free. But receiving that gift will change your life.

Grace That Transforms

There's a dangerous message in the world today—one that twists grace into a license to sin. It says, "Since I'm saved by grace, my actions don't matter. I can live however I want."

That's not biblical grace. That's deception.

Titus 2:11–12 (KJV) tells us exactly what grace does:

"For the grace of God that bringeth salvation hath appeared to all men, teaching us that, denying ungodliness and worldly lusts, we should live soberly, righteously,

39

and godly, in this present world."

Real grace doesn't make you comfortable in sin—it teaches you to walk away from it. It changes your appetite. It renews your mind. It stirs your heart to live holy—not to earn Heaven, but to reflect the One who bought your ticket there.

Faith Without Fruit?

We are not saved *by* works. But the Bible is clear—we are saved *unto* good works.

James 2:17–18 (KJV):

"Even so faith, if it hath not works, is dead, being alone. Yea, a man may say, Thou hast faith, and I have works: shew me thy faith without thy works, and I will shew thee my faith by my works."

In other words, your works are the evidence of your faith. The fruit of your life proves the root of your heart.

You May Be the Only Bible They Read

We live in a world that is watching. Some people may never open a Bible. But they're reading *you.* Your attitude. Your reactions. Your conversations. Your choices. The way you carry yourself under pressure. The way you love the unlovable. The way you hold onto hope when the world is falling apart.

It all matters.

Matthew 5:16 (KJV):

"Let your light so shine before men, that they may see your good works, and glorify your Father which is in heaven."

Let's be honest—when people look at your life, do they see the light... or just another flicker?

Not to Earn, But to Shine

Let's be clear:

- Your church attendance won't save you.
- Your giving won't get you in the gates.
- Your good deeds don't buy Heaven.

Only the blood of Jesus saves. Only grace can redeem. But once that grace hits your life, you should never be the same again.

Ephesians 2:8–10 (KJV):

"For by grace are ye saved through faith; and that not of yourselves: it is the gift of God: Not of works, lest any man should boast. For we are his workmanship, created in Christ Jesus unto good works, which God hath before ordained that we should walk in them."

Heaven is free—but discipleship is costly. It costs your comfort, your pride, your sin, your self.

But what you gain in return—peace, purpose, power, eternal life—is worth far more.

Living Like We're Already There

If Heaven lives in you, it should show.

Not in perfection, but in direction.

Not in pride, but in humility.

Not in spotlight, but in salt and light.

You don't work for salvation—But your life should work *because* of it.

Let the fruit of your life speak loudly.

Let the fire of grace burn brightly.

Let your walk preach louder than your words ever could.

Because someone, somewhere, is watching. And what they see in you might just lead them to the same Jesus who saved you.

Heaven is free. But it's not cheap.

Live like it cost something—because it did.

"This world is lost, broken, and deceived. People are drowning in fear, confusion, addiction, identity crisis, depression, and anxiety. And here we are— with the answer."

8
Chapter Eight
Shouting from the Rooftops

If I told you the building you were standing in was on fire, would I whisper it?

Would I wait for the perfect moment? Would I carefully calculate how not to offend you—or would I shout to save your life?

When you know something is true... and when you know someone's life depends on it... *you don't stay silent.*

And yet that's exactly what many believers do with the greatest truth of all time: **Jesus is coming soon.**

We say we believe in Heaven and Hell. We say we believe that people must be saved. We say we believe in eternity.

But if we really believed it, wouldn't we be shouting from the rooftops?

What Are We Afraid Of?

Jesus didn't call us to comfort—He called us to proclaim. Yet so many believers stay quiet out of fear of judgment, rejection, or discomfort. But Jesus was clear:

Matthew 10:27 (KJV):

"What I tell you in darkness, that speak ye in light: and what ye hear in the ear, that preach ye upon the housetops."

We've been entrusted with truth that can change lives, heal hearts, and save souls. And we're treating it like a private opinion rather than a public declaration.

The early church turned the world upside down—because they opened their mouths.

If We Stay Silent, Stones Will Speak

When Jesus entered Jerusalem riding on a donkey, people began to praise Him openly. The religious leaders told Jesus to rebuke them.

His response?

Luke 19:40 (KJV):

"I tell you that, if these should hold their peace, the stones would immediately cry out."

This isn't the hour to be quiet. Creation itself is groaning. Prophecy is unfolding. The world is spinning toward final judgment. And too many Christians are busy *watching* the signs but not *warning* others.

We Are the Watchmen

God spoke clearly to Ezekiel:

Ezekiel 33:6 (KJV):

"But if the watchman see the sword come, and blow not the trumpet, and the people be not warned; if the sword come, and take any person from among them,
 he is taken away in his iniquity; but his blood will I require at the watchman's hand."

We are not just called to *know* the truth. We are called to *sound the alarm.*

You don't need a pulpit. You don't need a title. You just need a voice—and the courage to use it.

Time Is Short

The reason we must speak now is because soon, we won't have the chance.

The trumpet will sound. The rapture will happen. And the moment for warnings will be over.

John 9:4 (KJV):

"I must work the works of him that sent me, while it is day: the night cometh, when no man can work."

You don't have forever. Neither do the people around you. Speak up while there's still light.

A World Dying for Truth

This world is lost, broken, and deceived. People are drowning in fear, confusion, addiction, identity crisis, depression, and anxiety. And here we are—with the answer.

His name is Jesus.

Romans 10:14 (KJV):

"How then shall they call on him in whom they have not believed? And how shall they believe in him of whom they have not heard? And how shall they hear without a preacher?"

You may not have a stage. But you have a story. And that story could be someone's rescue.

Don't Let Fear Win

Hell wants you to stay silent.

Heaven wants you to speak boldly.

And the world needs to hear it—before it's too late.

Let your life speak. Let your mouth declare. Let your faith rise.

The message is urgent.

The time is short.

And the rooftops are waiting.

Shout it loud. Shout it clear. Jesus is coming soon.

"Don't Miss That Moment. This is what it's all been about. Not escaping earth. Not avoiding wrath. But being with Him."

9
Chapter Nine
When Belief Becomes Sight

We've believed for years. Prayed with eyes closed. Worshipped a Savior we've never seen. Held fast to promises spoken centuries ago—because faith told us they were true. But there's coming a moment…When the One we've believed in will stand before us. And the unseen will become *undeniable*.

That moment will change everything.

Faith Has a Destination
We often think of faith as something we live with forever. But faith is only for this side of eternity. On the other side… **faith becomes sight.**

2 Corinthians 5:7 (KJV):
"(For we walk by faith, not by sight:)"

But when we see Jesus face to face, the walk of faith ends at the feet of glory. The One we trusted in the dark will be shining in the light.

All the doubts… gone.
All the questions… silenced.
All the tears… wiped away.

The Glorious Appearing

The rapture isn't just a rescue—it's a reunion. We're not just leaving earth. We're going to meet a Person.

1 John 3:2 (KJV):

"Beloved, now are we the sons of God, and it doth not yet appear what we shall be: but we know that, when he shall appear, we shall be like him; for we shall see him as he is."

Can you imagine that moment?

The trumpet sounds. The dead in Christ rise. We who are alive are changed in an instant. And suddenly, we see Him—not in vision, not in Scripture, but **as He is.**

Eyes like fire.

Face shining like the sun.

Voice like many waters.

Hands that still bear the marks of love.

From Believing to Beholding

Your entire walk with Jesus—every prayer, every step, every moment of faith—has been leading to this one encounter.

Job 19:25–27 (KJV):

"For I know that my redeemer liveth, and that he shall stand at the latter day upon the earth: And though after my skin worms destroy this body, yet in my flesh shall I see God: Whom I shall see for myself, and mine eyes shall behold, and not another…"

What Job hoped for in ashes—we will experience in glory.

Words Will Fail

We think we know what we'll do. We imagine we'll shout, dance, or fall to our knees.

But truthfully? That kind of holiness… that kind of beauty… that kind of love… Our earthly bodies won't be able to bear it.

We will be changed.

Philippians 3:20–21 (KJV):
"For our conversation is in heaven; from whence also we look for the Saviour, the Lord Jesus Christ: Who shall change our vile body, that it may be fashioned like unto his glorious body…"

No more pain.

No more fear.

No more separation between us and our Savior.

The Fulfillment of Everything

All the waiting… worth it.

All the warfare… won.

All the longing… satisfied.

We won't need faith anymore—because we'll be standing in the presence of the One we trusted.

Revelation 22:4 (KJV):
"And they shall see his face; and his name shall be in their foreheads."

Not just forgiven—*face to face.*

Don't Miss That Moment

This is what it's all been about.

Not escaping earth. Not avoiding wrath.

But being with **Him.**

The One who died for you.

The One who's prepared a place for you.

The One who's coming again to receive you.

And when you see Him…

You'll realize every ounce of belief you ever had wasn't even close to what He truly is.

He is worthy. He is coming. And when belief becomes sight… eternity begins.

"I pray that you'll be one of the ones caught up in the clouds, not left behind in the chaos."

10
Chapter Ten
The Invitation

You've made it to the end of this book, but this doesn't have to be the end of your story. In fact, it might just be the beginning.

I need to share something with you—something very important. One day in the near future, the world will wake up and ask:

"Where have all the people gone?"

They were just here a moment ago.

That man on YouTube who warned about the Rapture in great detail? Gone. No new videos. His account seems to be deactivated—flagged by fact-checkers as "misinformation."

That sweet lady who always tried to tell me about Jesus, even when I was too busy to listen? She's gone too.

That kind man who always gave so freely, who helped without asking? Missing.

The local food bank—always there when I needed help? Closed. Doors locked. No plans to reopen.

Where have all the truly kind people gone?

One day soon, these will be the words uttered by those left behind. A global vanishing will shake the world, and the common thread among the missing will be clear: **They had Jesus in their hearts.**

The kindness they carried wasn't just personality or habit—it was a byproduct of Christ living in them. And when Christ took His people home, that light left with them.

After the Rapture, much of the world's goodness will vanish. Why? Because what remained of decency was upheld by the faithful remnant—*and that remnant will be gone.*

The Greatest Revival After the Greatest Departure

What will be left behind is a broken, chaotic world. And yet, even then, God will not stop reaching. A great revival will spring up—not from churches, but from the *fringes.*

These will be the doubting Thomases. The ones who needed to *see* to believe. People who once heard the truth but denied the power of it.

They'll see Revelation unfold before their eyes.

They'll remember what they were told. And many will finally believe.

These new believers—**the tribulation saints**—will walk in faith, but also in unimaginable suffering. They'll learn what persecution truly is. Their path will be narrow, painful, and costly.

If you are reading this before the Rapture—you still have time to avoid that path.

Why Wait?

If you believe in Jesus, don't wait another second. Confess Him as Lord. Invite Him into your life. Turn from sin and follow Him. Not just in word, but in action.

Romans 10:9 (KJV):

"That if thou shalt confess with thy mouth the Lord Jesus, and shalt believe in thine heart that God hath raised him from the dead, thou shalt be saved."

If you're reading this after the Rapture…Yes, it's going to be hard. Horrific, even. But it's not hopeless.

You *can* still come to Christ. You *can* still be saved. But your life will never be the same. Persecution will be real. Your faith will be tested like never before.

The First Trip or the Last Chance

The Rapture is the first trip—the escape before the storm. The second coming of Jesus happens after the seven-year tribulation, and those years will be filled with darkness, destruction, and despair.

Few will survive.

Why would you risk going through that when Jesus is offering you eternal life—**now**?

Jesus said in **Luke 21:36 (KJV):**

"Watch ye therefore, and pray always, that ye may be accounted worthy to escape all these things that shall come to pass, and to stand before the Son of man."

This is your moment.

Don't wait to see if it all comes true. Don't be the one searching the news, confused, saying, *"They were right... and now it's too late."*

Wake Up Before It's Too Late

You can read the book of Revelation, or you can live it. Reading it will shake you. Living it will break you.

Let this be your wake-up call. Revelation isn't just prophecy anymore—it's becoming reality. Every day, we're getting deeper into the chapters.

We are the generation that can turn on the news and then open the Bible and see the same events side by side.

We are seeing prophecy fulfilled before our eyes—more now than at any other time in human history. **Time is short.**

And God has raised up Watchmen to sound the alarm. Not because they're special—but because they've been paying attention. They see the season. They know what time it is. And they're shouting the warning while there's still breath in their lungs.

You Still Have Time—But Not Much

You don't have to go through the Tribulation. You don't have to wonder if you're saved. You don't have to be left behind.

If you know Jesus—live like He's coming today. If you don't know Him—come to Him now.

Here's a simple prayer to guide you:

Lord Jesus, I believe You are the Son of God.
I believe You died for my sins and rose again.
I confess that I need You. Forgive me.
Come into my life. Be my Lord and Savior.
Help me to live for You every day.
I want to be ready when You return.
Thank You for saving me. In Jesus' name, Amen.

If you prayed that and meant it—welcome home.

You're no longer who you used to be.

You're forgiven.

You're His.

Final Words Before the Trumpet Sounds

I pray that you'll be one of the ones caught up in the clouds, not left behind in the chaos. I pray you'll hear the trumpet—not as a shock, but as a song of deliverance. I pray you'll say *"This is it!"*—and not *"Why didn't I listen?"*

Because once the Rapture takes place… What comes next is too much to bear. And why endure what you can escape?

Jesus is coming soon.

The warnings are here.

The time is now.

This is it.

Be ready.

In-Depth
Reflections

GOD, WHAT'S THE HOLD UP?

Chapter One
The Dream That Shook Me

Theme: *The rapture is real. Are you ready?*

Key Takeaways:
- God still speaks through dreams (see Joel 2:28).
- The rapture will be sudden and unmistakable.
- Transformation into our glorified body is promised to every believer.

Key Scriptures (KJV):
- **1 Thessalonians 4:16–17**

"For the Lord himself shall descend from heaven with a shout... and so shall we ever be with the Lord."

- **1 Corinthians 15:52**

"In a moment, in the twinkling of an eye, at the last trump... and we shall be changed."

- **Luke 21:36**

"Watch ye therefore, and pray always, that ye may be accounted worthy to escape..."

Reflection Questions:

1. If Jesus came back today, are you confident you would be taken?

2. Are you spiritually alert, or spiritually distracted?

3. What distractions do you need to surrender in order to live ready?

Chapter Two
When the Bible Looks Like the News

Theme: *Prophecy is not future fiction—it's present reality.*

Key Takeaways:
- We are living in a time that mirrors 2 Timothy 3.
- God's Word is unfolding right before our eyes.
- The signs are not just warnings—they're invitations to wake up.

Key Scriptures (KJV):
- **2 Timothy 3:1–5**

"This know also, that in the last days perilous times shall come…"

- **Matthew 24:6–8**

"And ye shall hear of wars and rumours of wars... All these are the beginning of sorrows."

- **Romans 13:11**

"It is high time to awake out of sleep: for now is our salvation nearer…"

Reflection Questions:

1. What current events have shaken your spirit and reminded you of prophecy?

2. Are you more focused on the world's chaos—or God's calling?

3. How can you help others connect the dots between the Bible and what's happening around them?

Chapter Three
The Chastisement Wake-Up Call

Theme: *God corrects those He loves.*

Key Takeaways:
- Chastisement is not punishment—it's a call back to relationship.
- Hard times often reveal the true posture of our hearts.
- God uses valleys to strip us of self and awaken us to His voice.

Key Scriptures (KJV):
- **Hebrews 12:6–7**

"For whom the Lord loveth he chasteneth... If ye endure chastening, God dealeth with you as with sons..."

- **Psalm 34:18**

"The Lord is nigh unto them that are of a broken heart..."

- **Deuteronomy 8:2**

"...to humble thee, and to prove thee, to know what was in thine heart..."

- **Revelation 3:19**

"As many as I love, I rebuke and chasten: be zealous therefore, and repent."

Reflection Questions:

1. Have you seen God use difficult moments to draw you closer to Him?

2. Are you resisting or responding to His correction?

3. How can you shift from asking "Why me?" to "What is God doing in me?"

Chapter Four
Pre-Tribulation Hope

Theme: *God has not appointed us to wrath.*

Key Takeaways:
- The rapture precedes the tribulation—it's our blessed hope.
- God's character is consistent—He delivers the righteous before judgment.
- The promise of escape is not a license to be lazy—it's a call to be ready.

Key Scriptures (KJV):
- **1 Thessalonians 4:16–17**

"Then we which are alive and remain shall be caught up… to meet the Lord in the air."

- **1 Thessalonians 5:9**

"For God hath not appointed us to wrath, but to obtain salvation…"

- **Revelation 3:10**

"I also will keep thee from the hour of temptation…"

- **Luke 21:36**

"Pray always, that ye may be accounted worthy to escape all these things…"

- **Titus 2:13**

"Looking for that blessed hope, and the glorious appearing…"

Reflection Questions:

1. How does knowing Jesus could return at any moment shape your daily decisions?

2. Are you living with hope—or fear?

3. Who in your life needs to hear about this hope?

Chapter Five
What Will Happen During the Tribulation

Theme: *Judgment coming—but God's mercy still reaches.*

Key Takeaways:
- The tribulation will be a time of unimaginable global suffering.
- God's wrath is righteous—and still wrapped in mercy for those who repent.
- Tribulation saints will rise, but their road will be one of sacrifice and persecution.

Key Scriptures (KJV):
- **Matthew 24:21**

"For then shall be great tribulation, such as was not since the beginning…"

- **2 Thessalonians 2:3–4**

"…that man of sin be revealed… so that he as God sitteth in the temple of God…"

- **Revelation 6, 8, 9, 13, 16** *(overview passages of seals, trumpets, and vials)*

- **Revelation 13:16–17**

"…no man might buy or sell, save he that had the mark…"

- **Isaiah 55:6**

"Seek ye the Lord while he may be found…"

- **2 Corinthians 6:2**

"…now is the accepted time; behold, now is the day of salvation."

Reflection Questions:

1. Do you feel a deeper urgency to share your faith after understanding what's coming?

2. How can you live differently in light of the wrath that Jesus saves us from?

3. Are there people you've given up on who may still turn to Christ—even after the rapture?

**Chapter Six
This Is Not a Drill**

Theme: *The warnings are real—and time is short.*

Key Takeaways:

- The world is not experiencing random chaos—it's a divine countdown.

- Complacency is dangerous. Spiritual snooze buttons could cost eternity.

- The trumpet won't come with a second warning. You must already be ready.

Key Scriptures (KJV):
- **Romans 13:11**

"...now it is high time to awake out of sleep: for now is our salvation nearer than when we believed."

- **Proverbs 27:1**

"Boast not thyself of to morrow; for thou knowest not what a day may bring forth."

- **Matthew 25:6–10**

"...they that were ready went in with him to the marriage: and the door was shut."

- **2 Peter 3:3–4**

"…There shall come in the last days scoffers… Where is the promise of his coming?"

- **John 9:4**

"I must work the works of him that sent me, while it is day…"

Reflection Questions:

1. What spiritual "snooze buttons" have you been hitting?

2. What does being "ready" look like in your life?

3. If the door shut today, would you be on the inside or outside?

In-Depth Reflections

Chapter Seven
Heaven Is Free—But Not Cheap

Theme: *Grace is free, but it should change everything about us.*

Key Takeaways:

- Salvation is a gift, but our lives should reflect the One who gave it.

- Works don't save us, but they reveal the authenticity of our faith.

- Your life may be the only Bible some people ever read—what is it saying?

Key Scriptures (KJV):

- **Romans 6:23**

"For the wages of sin is death; but the gift of God is eternal life…"

- **Titus 2:11–12**

"For the grace of God… Teaching us that… we should live soberly, righteously…"

- **James 2:17–18**

"…faith, if it hath not works, is dead… I will shew thee my faith by my works."

- **Matthew 5:16**

"Let your light so shine before men, that they may see your good works…"

- **Ephesians 2:8–10**

"For by grace are ye saved through faith… created in Christ Jesus unto good works…"

Reflection Questions:

1. What do your actions say about the grace that saved you?

2. In what ways are you being salt and light to the people around you?

3. How can you let your life preach Christ without saying a word?

Chapter Eight
Shouting from the Rooftops

Theme: *The world needs to hear what we know.*

Key Takeaways:
- Silence is not an option when eternity is on the line.

- You don't need a pulpit—just a voice and boldness.

- If we truly believe what we say we believe, we should be proclaiming it.

Key Scriptures (KJV):
- **Matthew 10:27**

"…what ye hear in the ear, that preach ye upon the housetops."

- **Luke 19:40**

"If these should hold their peace, the stones would immediately cry out."

- **Ezekiel 33:6**

"…if the watchman see the sword come, and blow not the trumpet… his blood will I require at the watchman's hand."

- **John 9:4**

"The night cometh, when no man can work."

- **Romans 10:14**

"…how shall they believe in him of whom they have not heard?"

Reflection Questions:

1. What is holding you back from speaking up for Christ?

2. Who in your life needs to hear the gospel while there's still time?

3. What can you do this week to become a louder rooftop voice?

Chapter Nine
When Belief Becomes Sight

Theme: *One day, faith will give way to glory.*

Key Takeaways:
- Our walk of faith is leading to a real moment—seeing Jesus face to face.

- Our earthly minds cannot comprehend the glory of that encounter.

- When we finally see Him, every sacrifice, prayer, and moment of belief will be worth it.

Key Scriptures (KJV):
- **2 Corinthians 5:7**

"(For we walk by faith, not by sight:)"

- **1 John 3:2**

"...we shall be like him; for we shall see him as he is."

- **Job 19:25–27**

"...yet in my flesh shall I see God: Whom I shall see for myself..."

- **Philippians 3:20–21**

"...Who shall change our vile body, that it may be fashioned like unto his glorious body..."

- **Revelation 22:4**

"And they shall see his face…"

Reflection Questions:

1. What does it mean to you to one day *see* the One you've believed in?

2. How does that day motivate your life today?

3. What distractions are pulling your eyes off the prize?

Chapter Ten
The Invitation

Theme: *Today is the day of salvation.*

Key Takeaways:
- The Rapture will be real—and permanent. The door will shut.

- If you're reading this now, you still have time to respond.

- Don't gamble with eternity. Come to Jesus now.

Key Scriptures (KJV):
- **Romans 10:9**

"That if thou shalt confess with thy mouth the Lord Jesus... thou shalt be saved."

- **Ephesians 2:8–9**

"For by grace are ye saved through faith... not of works..."

- **2 Corinthians 6:2**

"...behold, now is the accepted time; behold, now is the day of salvation."

- **Luke 21:36**

"...pray always, that ye may be accounted worthy to escape..."

- **Matthew 25:10**

"…and the door was shut."

Reflection Questions:

1. Have you truly surrendered your life to Christ?

2. If not, what are you waiting for?

3. Who do you know that still needs to hear this message—and how will you tell them?

If you like this book you will love this...

Up, Up, and Away with Jesus:
In a blink, the day Jesus comes to take us home

This book invites young readers on a heartfelt journey to understand the rapture of the church through the relatable perspective of a child. This book gently explains Jesus' promise to take those who trust Him to a wonderful place called Heaven—a place filled with endless joy, peace, and love.

With simple language and comforting assurance, children will learn about the exciting day Jesus may return, as described in the Bible. They'll discover how placing their trust in Jesus and following Him leads to a life filled with purpose and a forever home with Him.

Through this inspiring story, kids are encouraged to embrace their faith, pray to Jesus, read the Bible, and share His love. A message of hope, joy, and God's unfailing promises, Up, Up, and Away with Jesus will leave every child eager to look forward to the most amazing adventure of all.

Perfect for families, Sunday schools, and anyone seeking to share the hope of Heaven with the little ones they love.

Learn more:
www.itsnotsorandom.com/books

Take a journey through the Gospels...

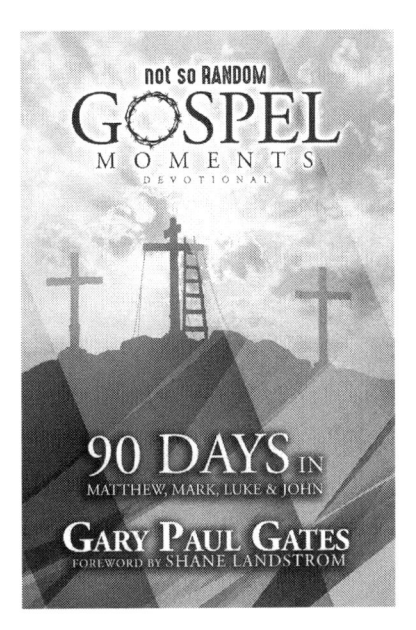

Not So Random Gospel Moments Devotional
90 Days in Matthew, Mark, Luke & John

Discover the Life of Jesus in 90 Days with Not So Random Gospel Moments

Have you ever wondered why the story of Jesus is told four times in the Bible? Not So Random Gospel Moments is a 90-day devotional designed to guide you through the Gospels of Matthew, Mark, Luke, and John—one chapter at a time.

Each day includes a Scripture reading, key takeaways, and insights to help you deepen your understanding of Christ's life, teachings, death, and resurrection. Whether you're new to the Gospels or seeking a fresh perspective, this journey will strengthen your faith and illuminate the richness of God's Word.

Take the challenge. Spend 90 days with Jesus. Be transformed.

Learn more:
www.itsnotsorandom.com/books

This is my testimony...

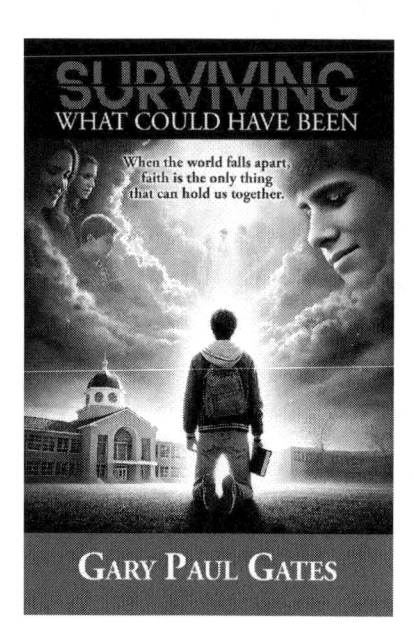

Surviving What Could Have Been
When the world falls apart, faith is the only thing that can hold us together

Gary Paul Gates' testimony, "Surviving What Could Have Been," is a personal reflection on his childhood leading into his high school years, drawing parallels to the tragic events at Columbine High School and the impact they had on him. The book is inspired by the story of Rachel Joy Scott, the first student killed at Columbine, and the author's realization that his own experiences were not as unique as he once believed.

Gates recounts his personal journey, sharing stories and thoughts that have never been publicly disclosed before. He explores the challenges and anxieties he faced as a teenager, including a sense of foreboding about the future. The book serves as a testament to the guidance and presence of God in his life, even during the darkest of times.

Learn more:
www.itsnotsorandom.com/books

God encounters, dreams, visions...

Not So Random Encounters
Stories of Faith, Kindness, and Miracles

Not So Random Encounters: Stories of Faith, Kindness, and Miracles is a collection of heartwarming and faith-filled stories that illustrate how God's hand works through the most ordinary moments of our lives. Whether it's through prophetic dreams, spontaneous acts of kindness, or divine guidance, these stories reveal the power of listening to God's voice and stepping out in faith.

Join the author Gary Paul Gates on a journey of personal encounters where the simple act of obedience leads to profound blessings, healing, and connection. From uplifting a struggling waitress to recreating a beloved family recipe, each story serves as a reminder that no act of kindness is ever random when it's directed by God.

Whether you're looking for encouragement in your faith or inspiration to make a difference in someone's life, Not So Random Encounters will challenge you to trust God's perfect timing and step into the miracles waiting around the corner.

Learn more:
www.itsnotsorandom.com/books

Made in the USA
Columbia, SC
25 June 2025